U. S. Army, Dept. of the Gulf, Bureau of Free Labor, Thomas
W. Conway

The Freedmen of Louisiana

Final report of the Bureau of Free Labor, Department of the Gulf, to Major

General E.R.S. Canby

U. S. Army, Dept. of the Gulf, Bureau of Free Labor, Thomas W. Conway

The Freedmen of Louisiana
Final report of the Bureau of Free Labor, Department of the Gulf, to Major General E.R.S. Canby

ISBN/EAN: 9783337285630

Printed in Europe, USA, Canada, Australia, Japan

Cover: Foto ©Andreas Hilbeck / pixelio.de

More available books at **www.hansebooks.com**

THE FREEDMEN OF LOUISIANA.

FINAL REPORT

OF THE

BUREAU OF FREE LABOR,

DEPARTMENT OF THE GULF,

TO

MAJOR GENERAL E. R. S. CANBY,

COMMANDING:

BY

THOMAS W. CONWAY,

GENERAL SUPERINTENDENT OF FREEDMEN.

PRINTED AT THE NEW ORLEANS TIMES BOOK AND JOB OFFICE.

1865.

REPORT.

HEADQUARTERS, BUREAU OF REFUGEES, FREEDMEN
AND ABANDONED LANDS, STATE OF LOUISIANA.
New Orleans, La., July 1st, 1865.

MAJOR GENERAL E. R. S. CANBY,
  Commanding Department of the Gulf :

GENERAL.—I beg leave to respectfully present a final report of the affairs of the Bureau of Free Labor, Department of the Gulf, prior to its transfer to the Bureau of Refugees, Freedmen and Abandoned Lands, over which Major General O. O. Howard presides.

THE WORK.

The Bureau commenced the year with a stupendous work before it, and without funds. Thousands of destitute freedmen came through our lines, at all points, and were forwarded by military commanders to me to be cared for and furnished with employment. I had to procure everything by purchase, medicines could not be procured of the purveyor, rations could, at one time, only be had by payment of cash for them, clothing had to be purchased, excepting some lots of deceased soldiers' clothing, turned over to me by the Quartermaster. I had to secure and stock, for the use of vagrant and helpless freedmen, four

HOME COLONIES.

At least thirty thousand dollars was required for that purpose.

During the year there have been under the control of the Bureau four Home Colonies. These are as follows, viz :

  The McHatton Home Colony, at Baton Rouge.

  The Rost and McCutcheon Home Colony, Parish of St. Charles.

  The Gen. Bragg Home Colony, Parish of Lafourche.

  The Sparks Home Colony, Parish of Jefferson.

The following tabular statement is annexed, as showing several items which may prove of interest :

REPORT OF FREEDMEN ON GOVERNMENT HOME COLONIES.

NAME OF COLONY.	Number of Acres.	DEPENDENTS. WELL. Males	Females	Children Males	Children Females	Total	SICK. Males	Females	Total	Total sick and well.	FOR GOVERNMENT. Cotton	Corn	Cane	Rattoon Cane	Garden Vegetables	Sweet Potatoes	For Corn broken up.	FOR FREEDMEN. Cotton	Corn	Miscellaneous	Estimated Value of Crop Produced.
McHatton	3000	65	110	105	115	395	103	112	215	640	140	186	11					60	100	130	$175,000
Bragg	2950	40	46	76	86	218	57	93	150	398	60	83			12	5				180	
Ross & McCutcheon	3000	113	114	107	115	452	51	97	148	600	220	530	132	210			100	250	140		
Sparks	700	87	34	35	49	198	15	51	66	264	220	200	143	210	12	5	100	210	240	310	
Total	9650	305	304	323	361	1293	226	383	609	1902	610	1019	143	210		10	100				

NOTE.—By terms of contract the Government is to receive one-third of the crops of lands cultivated by freedmen.

NOTE.—The plantations formerly in charge of the Treasury Department are in many cases worked on shares, the Government having a fractional part of the crop. The proceeds from this source will also accrue to the benefit of the Bureau.

NOTE.—The number of acres of the Sparks' place, as set forth above, alludes only to the cleared land.

NOTE.—The Government has, by the terms of agreement with Mr. Sparks, a first lien upon the property for expenses.

Much surprise may be manifested at the apparently large number of sick reported ; but it must be borne in mind that the main object in view, in the establishment of these colonies, was to provide a place of refuge and a *home* for the aged and helpless freedmen, thrown upon the Bureau for support. The crops are in good condition, and the farms are managed as successfully as if in the hands of private parties. The Sparks Home Colony was worked by its proprietor for some months, but being unable to work it further, he turned it into my hands. This place being close to New Orleans, and well adapted to the wants of the Bureau, furnishing a ready place of refuge to the vagrants of the city, who were constantly being thrown upon my hands by the military and civil authorities, and the large numbers of helpless freedmen who were also flocking to me for help, made its acquisition very desirable. I previously held the Belleville Iron Foundry, at Algiers, as a place of asylum for these characters, but as I had no means of furnishing them with employment, the plantation of Mr. Sparks was most acceptable. I desired to impress upon the minds of all who came into my charge that work could in no case be avoided, and that if they fell upon the Government to be maintained, they must work as hard as if they were employed by contract on the plantation of any private citizen. The fact that while in my charge they must work as hard as if employed by others, and get no pay, has been instrumental in decreasing the number of vagrants who would otherwise have crowded upon me.

In these establishments labor is forced, and none can avoid it, unless they are physically unable to perform it. All contribute something to the support of themselves and their families. These colonies are well organized. Each has a superintendent, a physician, a cultivator of the land and a clerk. There is now, in good condition, at each of them, a school for instruction in the common English branches, a Sunday school for moral and religious training, and, where the parties have so desired, there are regularly organized churches.

My plan has been to render them self-supporting. The crops now growing will reimburse the Government for all outlays. It has been determined not to allow the work of caring for the freedmen of the Department to be of any expense whatever to the United States, and, from the present appearance of the crops, I am quite certain I will be able to show that my hopes in this respect will be fully realized.

Considered in every way, I regard the Home Colonies as a most successful feature in the government and care of freedmen. Indeed without them the crime of vagrancy would prevail to a great extent, and go unpunished and unchecked.

VAGRANCY.

At no time have I had more than four hundred persons who could be properly classed as vagrants. This number is less, by many thousands, than was generally supposed to have been supported by this Bureau. I find that the colored people are not apt to be vagrants. They have fewer vagrants than can be found among any other class of persons, and by far the fewest beggars. The largest number in my charge are helpless persons, old men, women and small children. The class usually called "vagrants" by the police and the courts are industrious and self-supporting.

PERSECUTIONS BY THE POLICE.

The injustice inflicted upon the freedmen at the hands of the New Orleans police, can hardly find its equal in the history of any city in Christendom.

It has been the practice here to arrest as vagrants all colored laborers who were found on the streets in their working garments, and not employed just at the moment when the police saw them. These men may have had as honest employment as their persecutors; they may have worked all day long in the burning sun, loading or unloading ships or boats; they may have been in the employ of the Quartermaster's Department, or some other Department of the Government; they may have their cotton hooks hanging to their belts, showing that they have proper employment; but still they have been arrested, locked up in jail and arraigned before the courts charged with the crime of vagrancy. Not a day passes without dozens of men being sent to me as vagrants, many of whom I release immediately upon ascertaining that they have been arrested unjustly. Those who are found to be vagrants are readily and effectively corrected at our colonies, where they are made to labor and contribute to the support of the helpless of their race. The troubles inflicted by the police, when reported to the Department Commander, were promptly checked.

THE SYSTEM OF LABOR.

Allow me to give you a statement of the condition of the country since February 1st, when the contract year commenced.

At that time the question of labor was the one which was the most generally discussed by planters and merchants. The failure of the crops last year, by the ravages of the army worm, was lost sight of when men talked about labor. The alleged idleness and insubordination of the negroes were always quoted as the cause of the failure. Newspapers and newspaper letter writers quoted the failure as proof positive that free labor was a failure. The gross crop was compared with that of other years, and the conclusion generally drawn was, that the present system of labor was a failure. This conclusion was heralded far and wide, and many thoughtless men were found ready to admit the force of the statement. It was not difficult to show, that at no time in the history of Louisiana had the planters so bright a prospect of large and profitable benefits from their investments as in 1864.

Great as was the supposed failure of the labor plan, it has produced a crop on about one thousand plantations, of all sizes, worth at least thirty millions of dollars. Considering that the rebels had driven the best laborers from the territory formerly within the lines of our military occupation into Texas, and that the United States, by a series of harsh and sweeping conscriptions, had taken into the army nearly all who remained who were of proper age and condition ; and considering, too, that most of the planters entered upon the work faithless and doubtful, and that the laborers were the poorest of their class, the crop produced showed a triumph of the free labor system. It exceeded the expectations of all reasonable men, and showed the freedmen to be not idlers but industrious.

A crop worth twenty or thirty millions could not have been destroyed by the worm had it not been produced by the laborers. This is conclusive enough, and the best planters of the State have estimated the loss as even greater than that which I state.

Nevertheless it was agreed that the plan was a failure, and in order to secure a better, meetings were called, and held by various persons and at various times. The agents of the Treasury Department made their arrangements for the government of plantations. These arrangements were discussed by the planters and generally disliked.

THE MEETINGS OF THE PLANTERS.

Pursuant to a call from Hon. B. F. Flanders, Supervising Special Agent of the Treasury Department, Third Agency, a meeting of planters and others interested in planting assembled at the rooms of the Chamber of Commerce, on the evening of Monday, the 21st November, 1864, of which Judge Joshua Baker, of Terrebonne Parish, was elected chairman. A committee of two gentlemen from each parish was appointed " to draw up rules and regulations for the better administration of the plantations of Louisiana, and the management, payment and feeding of the freed laborers, and to suggest such changes in the regulations presented by the Secretary of the Treasury, under date of July 29. 1864, as they deemed of vital importance to the agriculture of the State."

A copy of these rules and suggestions was to be presented to an adjourned meeting, on Tuesday evening, the 22d November. The rules and suggestions were submitted, accepted by the planters, and their adoption urged. *Any of these, if approved and enforced, as desired, would have brought the freedmen again into bondage, in fact, if not in name.* It was surprising to behold men, of considerable intelligence, urge measures upon the attention of the authorities, which if allowed, would be in direct violation of the Proclamation of President Lincoln, giving liberty to the enslaved, and in open conflict with the ruling spirit of the Government.

They urged that for insolence, disobedience, improper behavior, or contempt of superiors, freedmen be punished by their employers, " as formerly." This last expression was so frequently used, that it was easily seen how devotedly they adhered to the old system of slavery. The better judgment of the former slaveholders of the State has at last gained the ascendancy, and now, as a general rule, the death of slavery is more widely acknowledged.

The following "suggestions" proposed at the meeting of the planters in this city, will illustrate the sentiment, which they entertained, at that time, toward the freedmen, and their idea of the manner in which they should be governed. •

They proposed :

"Some mode of compelling laborers to perform ten hours faithful work in each twenty-four hours (Sundays excepted) *and strict obedience of all orders.* This may be partially obtained by a graduated system of fines, deduction of time or wages, deduction of rations of all kinds in proportion to time lost, rigidly enforced ; but in obstinate cases, it can only be done by corporeal punishment, such as are inflicted in the Army and Navy of the United States. *In light cases of disobedience of orders, and non-performance of duty, the employer should impose fines, etc.*"

They proposed, also, that laborers should be held accountable for teams, carts, wagons, gear, tools, etc., of all kinds ; also, that parents be responsible and liable for articles stolen by their children—that "the unauthorized purchase of clothing, or other property, *by laborers, or others domesticated on plantations, should be severely punished ; and so should the sale, by laborers, or others domesticated on plantations, of plantation products, without a written permission, be punished by fine, imprisonment, and, in obstinate cases, by corporeal punishment.*"

They wound up one set of suggestions, announcing that "The whole study, aim and object of the negro laborer now is, how to avoid work, and yet have a claim for wages, rations, clothes, etc."

Another party proposes that—

"*No hand shall leave the plantation for the purpose of visiting or trading, without the permission of the employer. Forfeiture of one day's work shall be the penalty for each violation of this rule.*

"No hand shall be allowed to roam at will over the plantation, in the night—at half-past 9, P. M., the bell should be rung, and any hand found out of his or her quarters, after that hour, without proper excuse, shall be fined one day's work.

"No hand shall keep on the plantation, without the permission of the employer, any horse, mule, pig, or cattle. Forfeiture of the property to the informer should be the penalty for the violation of this rule. In case permission is given to keep hogs, they must be kept in pens. If caught running at large, they shall be forfeited.

"No hand shall cultivate any cotton or cane upon his own account. The land given him for a garden must be devoted to that use."

The committee to draft these rules was, as before stated, to consist of two gentlemen from each parish, and was composed as follows :

Messrs. Lessepps and Decker, of Plaquemines.
"   Walker and Knapp, of St. Bernard.
"   Urquhart and Degrét, of Orleans, right bank.
"   Wetmore and Osgood, of Jefferson.
"   Quick and Snow, of St. Charles.
"   Maimé and May, of St. John the Baptiste.

Messrs. Kock and Tillotson, of Ascension.
"   Pugh and Hunt, of Assumption.
"   Green and Perkins, of Lafourche Interior.
"   McCullum and Henderson, of Terrebonne.
"   Lawrence and Smith, of St. Mary.
"   Goodale and Jones, of East Baton Rouge.
"   Austin and Gay, of Iberville.

Those who urged that these measures be adopted, appeared to be entirely unaware of the fact, that they would bring anarchy to the country, and utter prostration to the planting interests themselves.

They lost sight of the fact, that though the freedmen are, as a general thing, not learned, they possess sufficient intelligence and good sense, to resolve never again to be reduced to slavery.

It was by adhering as closely as possible to the old system that the planters appeared to expect success; whereas, success depended more in a total abandonment of every feature of slavery, and a cordial adoption of the same system and rules of labor, as are found operating in any of the free States, accepting as a temporary necessity of the condition of the country, the safeguards established by the military authorities. This was done by the planters, but not voluntarily. The freedmen, on the other hand, would accept no arrangement which was not inspected and approved by some officer of the Government. In some cases, there was trouble growing out of the efforts of some employers to fasten upon the freedmen some obligations which would be prejudicial to their (the freedmen's) interests.

The planters were able to take advantage of the freedmen, and the freedmen, knowing this, distrusted them. Here was a root of bitterness which nothing could remedy, except the stern protecting arm of the Government. After considerable discussion and annoyance, growing out of the unsettled state of affairs, the labor arrangements of the Treasury Department were set aside, by Major Gen. S. A. Hurlbut, acting under instructions of the Major General commanding the Military Division of West Mississippi. Then arose the necessity of replacing the Treasury regulations by some other. General Hurlbut asked me for such a plan, in writing, as I thought would be practicable. I submitted such rules as long experience and an extensive knowledge of the wants of the country, enabled me to believe would answer every purpose. General Hurlbut had, by this time, prepared an order, similar in most respects to that which Major General N. P. Banks had issued the year previously. This order was issued, and appeared to give general satisfaction. Thus far, experience demonstrates its admirable adaptation to the necessities which surrounded us. ? The following is the Labor Order:

HEADQUARTERS, DEPARTMENT OF THE GULF,
New Orleans, March 11th, 1865.

GENERAL ORDERS }
No. 23. }

The Regulations heretofore published by Mr. W. P. MELLEN, General Agent Treasury Department, in relation to freedmen and labor, not having been recognized by the Secretary of the Treasury, the following orders are prescribed for the hiring and government of laborers within the State of Louisiana.

HOME COLONIES.

1. The Home Colonies, already established by Orders from these Headquarters, are hereby continued under said Orders.

SUPERINTENDENCY.

2. Mr. THOMAS W. CONWAY, as Superintendent, with such Assistants as he may designate, will be obeyed and respected by all persons in the discharge of their respective duties.

REGISTRY OF PLANTATIONS.

3. The system of Registry of Plantations, as prescribed in Mr. Mellen's Regulations and the Military Orders in relation thereto, will continue and be in force as therein required.

HIRE AND COMPENSATION OF LABORERS.

4. Voluntary contracts heretofore made between planters and laborers, or which hereafter may be made, will be submitted to the Superintendent of Freedmen, and if found by him to be fair and honest to the laborers, will be by him confirmed and approved, and stand as the contract of the parties thereto for the present year. But all such contracts must secure support, maintenance, clothing and medical attendance to the laborer.

5. The following schedule will be observed in all other cases, as the rule required by the Government.

In addition to just treatment, wholesome rations, comfortable clothing, quarters, fuel and medical attendance, and the opportunity for instruction of childen, the planter shall pay to the laborer as follows :

Male Hands—First Class, $10 per month.
Second Class, $8 per month.
Third Class, $6 per mouth.
Female Hands—First Class. $8 per month.
Second Class. $6 per month.
Third Class, $5 per month.
Boys under 14, $3 per month.
Girls under 14, $2 per month.

These classes will be determined by merit and on agreement between the planter and the laborers.

6. Engineers, foremen and mechanics will be allowed to make their own contracts, but will receive not less than $5 per month additional to first-class rates.

7. One-half of the money wages due will be paid quarterly, as follows : On the first days of May. August and November, and final payment of the entire amount then due, on or before the 31st day of January.

PENALTIES.

8. Wages for the time lost will be deducted in case of sickness ; and both wages and rations where the sickness is feigned for purposes of idleness ; and in cases of feigned sickness, or refusal to work according to contract, when able so to do, such offender will be reported by the Provost Marshal to the Superintendent, and put upon forced labor on public works, without pay.

The laborers must understand that it is their own interest to do their work faithfully, and that the Government, while it will protect and sustain them against ill-treatment, cannot support those who are capable of earning an honest living by industry.

9. Laborers will be allowed and encouraged to choose their own employers, but when they have once selected, they must fulfil their contract for the year, and will not be permitted to leave their place of employment, (except in cases where they are permitted so to do for just reasons, by the authority of the Superintendent,) and if they do so leave without cause and permission, they will forfeit all wages earned to the time of abandonment, and be otherwise punished, as the nature of the case may require.

10. Planters and their agents will be held to rigid accountability for their conduct towards the laborers, and any cruelty, inhumanity or neglect of duty will be summarily punished.

TIME OF LABOR AND PERQUISITES OF LABORERS.

11. The time of labor shall be ten hours, between daylight and dark in summer, and nine hours in winter, of each day, except Saturday and Sunday.

The afternoon of Saturday and the whole of Sunday shall be at the disposal of the laborer.

On sugar estates, at the proper season, the hands will take their regular watches, the night work of which, and the Saturday afternoons and Sundays, if positively necessary, shall be paid for as extra work.

Laborers will be allowed land for private cultivation at the following rates:

1st and 2d class hands, with families, one acre each.

1st and 2d class hands, without families, one-half acre each.

2d and 3d class hands, with families, one-half acre each.

2d and 3d class hands, without families, one-quarter acre each.

On these allotments they will be allowed to raise such crops as they may choose for their own use and benefit, but will not be permitted to raise or keep animals, except domestic poultry.

POLL TAX.

12. For the purpose of reimbursing to the United States some portion of the expenses of this system, and of supporting the aged, infirm and helpless, the following tax will be collected in lieu of all other claim under these Regulations:

From each planter, for every hand employed by him, between the ages of 18 and 50, two dollars per annum.

From each hand between the same ages, one dollar per annum.

This sum will be payable and be collected on the 1st day of June next, and will be paid over to the Superintendent of Freedmen, for disbursement.

Measures will be taken to collect the same Poll Tax from all colored persons not on plantations, so that the active labor of this race may contribute to the support of their own helpless and disabled.

GENERAL DUTIES.

13. Provost Marshals in the several parishes are charged with the general supervision and welfare of the laborers, reporting on these subjects frequently to Mr. T. W. Conway, Superintendent, and will use all possible exertion, by themselves and their deputies, to see that industry and good order are promoted, and that the contracts under these orders are faithfully performed by both parties. Orders heretofore issued and published, so far as they are not changed or modified by this order, will remain in force.

14. This order shall be deemed and taken to have effect from the 1st day of February last, and all contracts entered into in relation to the labors of the present year will be held to be controlled, amended and governed by the term and conditions of this order.

LIEN AND SECURITY FOR LABOR.

15. All crops and property on any plantation where laborers are employed will be held to be covered by a lien against all other creditors to the extent of the wages due employées, and such lien will follow such crops or property in any and all hands until such labor is fully paid and satisfied.

BY COMMAND OF MAJOR GENERAL HURLBUT:

GEORGE B. DRAKE,
Lieut. Col. and Assistant Adjutant General.

THE POLL TAX ORDERED, AND ITS COLLECTION.

One of the features of the order issued by Major General Hurlbut, was the levying of a tax of two dollars, from each planter, for each hand employed by him between the ages of eighteen and fifty ; and one dollar from each hand so employed. The tax from the hand to be paid by the employer and withheld from his wages.

This portion of the order was conceded to be just and proper by the planters, and their willingness to pay the same was generally expressed. It disposed of the enormous rents levied in the Treasury Regulations, for the support of the helpless and for military protection. Very soon, however, when the tax was being collected, it was generally condemned, and I am sorry to say, that among the foremost advocates of the change made by General Hurlbut, were men who subsequently offered the most opposition, alleging that the collection of a tax for the support of home colonies for old and helpless freedmen, was an oppression on the part of the Government, which they could not endure. Plain men, who had little or nothing to do with the rebellion, and who cared more for their farms than they did for politics, seldom make any objection to the measures of relief and employment, which the Government has found it necessary to adopt. The men, among the planters, who say the most about the oppression which they suffer, at the hands of the Government, are those who had sons in the rebel army as Colonels, Generals, etc. ; and, in not a few cases, those who complain most of the unsatisfactory labor of the freedmen, are men who pay their laborers unfairly, and who treat them with the most severity.

Up to the date of this report, about twenty thousand dollars of the poll tax has been collected, and payments are being made daily.

FREE LABOR AND ITS OPPONENTS.

Men who were strong rebels against the Government, are, almost invariably, strong opponents of free labor. They continually harp upon its impracticability, and are free in the utterance of opinions against it. They hire their laborers in a spirit of opposition to them, and to the system of labor which is adopted. When they pay them, they do so in an opposing spirit, which the freedmen understand to be opposition to their liberty. There are bright exceptions, of course. Men, whose hearts are not sufficiently softened to reconcile them to the change from slave to free labor, can hardly expect that the freedmen will be content to live with them and cultivate their soil. The freedmen are ready and anxious to work. They do not expect to be idle, but they do expect to have their employers recognize the fact that they are as free as others. Employers who show that they do recognize this, and who treat their laborers accordingly, have but little trouble.

The enemies of free labor claim that slave labor is superior. They do so, more because of the force of prejudice than because there are facts to justify them. In 1864, the crop was so good, within the military lines of the

United States, that planters, lessees, speculators, and others, thought they would make more money, in proportion to their investments, than ever before. Sugar and cotton were very valuable. The yield, up to the date of its destruction by the army worm, was very rich. All who were interested were pleased. The fact that many thousands of the best colored laborers had been taken into Texas, by their rebel owners ; and that several thousands of the able-bodied men, who remained, had been swept into the Union army, by a series of severe conscriptions, leaving only a very small proportion of the best laborers of the State, to cultivate the region then in our control, did not enter their minds, in the determination of their conclusions. The crops realized were good ; that is all they cared for. ⌐

THE DESTRUCTION OF THE CROP.

Soon the worm came. and soon afterwards the rich crop disappeared. Men worth hundreds of thousands were left not worth a hundred cents—merchants, brokers, speculators, and others, were ruined by the failure. Many a man ran away to his native clime, in some part of our own country, or to some other country, anxious never again to invest his hard earnings in the vain hope of " five hundred per cent. gain," by the rich yearly produce of the soil of Louisiana.

The failure of bad men was really a public benefit. There were, from some of the "free States," a class of men who cared nothing for humanity, nothing for religion. nothing for the Union, nothing for the army : they cared only for their pecuniary interests. These came to Louisiana, as ready to whip the freedmen, provided it would bring them gain to do so. as they were to condemn the same conduct on the part of the men who formerly owned the freedmen as their slaves. Anything to help them in making money. This way or that way, or any other way, only that money should come out of it. This was their character, this their purpose. To those, who were bending every energy to honestly and earnestly help the Government policy, these men were only a disgrace and a stumbling block. Southern men, who had owned the freedmen. pointed to *their* conduct, as proof that slavery was better for the negro than freedom. This was denied. on the ground that the vindication of liberty was to be left to the conduct of the liberated, and not to the treatment of speculators toward them.

This latter class have been of no benefit to the wise policy of our Government in the settlement of this difficult problem. If the vindication of the emancipation proclamation were left to their conduct, I should fail in even hoping to see a satisfactory solution of the problem, Its justice will not be shown by these, but by the freedmen themselves. ⌐

FREE LABOR AND ITS SUPPORTERS.

In justice to those Northern men who are now here—men who came with their wealth. with the intention of settling in the State ; who came with the love of the principles of liberty well fixed in their minds. I must say that they have set an example worthy of emulation. They are as ready to educate the freedmen as they are to employ them. They desire to see them morally, socially and politically elevated. Mention might be made of a few Southern men who manifested the same good sense ; as, for instance, Hon Thomas P. May, Assistant Treasurer of the United States. With these men the Bureau never has any trouble. If others would pay the freedmen as regularly and as fairly as they, we would have no difficulty.

THE PROSPECT IN THE FUTURE.

There is room for honest and sensible men—men who understand, in their own liberty, what the liberty of others should be, and who are not too proud to work, and are desirous of settling here as citizens. To such men a bright prospect presents itself. There are rich fields to be purchased at low rates. There can be plenty of labor to such as pay fairly for it. The profits are such as will sufficiently reward any one. If, in the precarious season of 1864, when the war was still raging, the inferior laborers left within the military lines, numbering less than thirty thousand, the others having been forced into Texas by the rebels, or into the United States army under military orders—if, under such circumstances, thirty millions of dollars could be derived from a crop produced in portions of a few parishes only, and with inferior work, what, I may ask, may we not expect with the ordinary labor of the State, under the influence of well regulated liberty, and of those elevating influences which free labor invariably calls to its own assistance?

I look for greater profits, and by far more happiness, to the white and colored populations of the State, under the influence of free labor, and in a very few years, than was ever before enjoyed. Instead of being always strangled with the enormous debts imposed upon planters by the slave system, I expect to see free labor bring planters into a condition of freedom from debt which will demonstrate the superiority of liberty.

ORPHAN ASYLUMS.

Three Orphan Asylums have been maintained in this city for the use of the Bureau in its care of the orphans of freedmen. These have been partially maintained by the colored people of the city of New Orleans ; and one of them, the one long organized by the Bureau on Dryades street, was placed in the exclusive charge of the National Freedmen's Relief Association, in order to secure better conduct of the establishment and economy to the Government. The Association has done very well in the care of the orphans committed to the Asylum. Another Asylum was organized in the Soulé mansion on Esplanade street, under the exclusive charge of Madame Louise De Mortié, an educated and philanthropic lady who came to the Department with letters of recommendation from some of the best citizens of New York and Boston. She was desirous of engaging in some philanthropic service, and fixed her attention upon an Orphan's Home for girls. Her object, when named to the Commanding General and myself, was approved, and her application for a suitable building was responded to by the assignment of the Soulé mansion for her purposes. This Asylum is conducted with but little expense to the Bureau, and is found to be very serviceable.

Two of the Asylums, the one established by the colored people themselves, and conducted by them without any direction from the Bureau, and the one long established by the Government, finding that they could accomplish more good by consolidation, united, and formed one Asylum, which is now in charge of the National Freedmen's Association, the Government furnishing the building, fuel and rations. These establishments have rendered great service. It was thought that five or ten thousand orphans of freedmen would be thrown upon our hands at the close of the war, but strange to say our numbers have hardly increased. I find the colored people themselves taking into their families the orphan children of their former friends or neighbors, thus saving us the necessity of bearing large expense in caring for them.

The colored people are often charged with lack of sympathy for each other, when in distress. My experience justifies me in saying that there is no ground for such a statement, but that on the contrary, they are kind to each other, and in many instances I have known them to assist their old masters when in trouble.

THE BREAKING UP OF THE MEETINGS OF THE FREEDMEN.

During the summer, the police of New Orleans have entered churches and broken up the meetings of humble Christian worshippers. So great appeared to be the antagonism exhibited by these men toward the liberty enjoyed by the colored population of the city, that they used their clubs upon the floors of the meeting-houses, creating such a noise as to break up the meetings and send the poor people home in a state of fright and discouragement. When the police were asked for their authority, they showed an order signed "J. Burke, Chief of Police," and upon further investigation, it was found that the Chief received his orders from the Mayor.

A positive order had to be given by the Commanding General to Hon. Hu. Kennedy, the Acting Mayor of New Orleans, before the churches belonging to the colored people could be allowed the same freedom enjoyed by white people. When it is considered that this order was called forth three years after the United States forces took possession of New Orleans, the temper of the inhabitants may be regarded as not very favorable, or very much improved ; and certainly the conduct of the authorities can be shown to be anything but encouraging. The following is the order about the Churches :

HEADQUARTERS, DEPARTMENT OF LOUISIANA AND TEXAS,
New Orleans, July 30, 1865.

The services in any church at this season, when the doors and windows are necessarily kept open, is probably an annoyance to sensitive and nervous persons who reside in the immediate neighborhood. I have known such complaints to be made of churches where the worshippers were white, but I have never known their worship to be tormented in the abrupt and discreditable manner in which it has been in the negro churches in this city, in several instances that have been reported to me.

The same rule will be applied, hereafter, to them as to other churches, and if the services in them have been conducted in such a manner as to furnish any real grounds of annoyance, measures will be taken by the Assistant Commissioner of Freedmen, to bring them under proper regulations and control.

E. R. S. CANBY,

Major General Commanding.

Rather than arrest the Chief of Police or any of his subordinates on account of such conduct, I preferred to call upon the Commanding General for help. My call was promptly responded to, and an order issued to the State authorities, and to the Mayor and Police of the city, directing that colored persons be treated with the same justice enjoyed by other people. Since the issue of that order, great improvement has been made, and now the colored people breathe more freely. There is, however, an occasional difficulty, arising more from the general antipathy which the police exhibit towards colored persons than from any orders of their superiors. The character of both State and city officials is pleasing to contemplate. I know of no other mischief done by the Governor in regard to the rights of the freedmen, than that which lies in his almost wholesale appointment of officers who, in their places, deal with the freedmen as if they wanted to deal with slaves rather than with free citizens. The conclusion which I am compelled to draw from the conduct of the State authorities towards the freedmen, is simply this : that if the freedmen were left to the mercy of the people who formerly owned them as slaves, or to officers of their selection, we might with one count of the fingers of our hands number the years which the race would spend with us.

DIVISION OF THE LANDS TO REFUGEES AND FREEDMEN.

Arrangements are already being made for the division of the abandoned and confiscable lands of Louisiana, to loyal refugees and freedmen, in pursuance of the law of Congress, Act March 3, 1865, and the orders of General Howard.

I find many applications from these people for lands on which they may settle and establish homesteads. Some freedmen apply who inform me that they have ten or fifteen thousand dollars with which to work the land which may be assigned them for their use ; others apply, stating that they have one, three or five thousand dollars at their command ; and others still, who apply and have nothing except that they are anxious to work land and give a share of the crops for advances. I find a disposition among the freedmen (which is almost universal) to have land given them for cultivation, for which they express themselves ready to pay as much rent as others.

During the year some plantations have been leased to freedmen, either individually or by associations; and I find that, considering their scanty means, they are working to good advantage. Through their savings and earnings for this and the past year, I expect to find enough of them to be able to cultivate through the coming year sixty thousand acres of land, lying chiefly on rivers or railroads, so as to give them the full benefit of the influences of trade, travel and commerce. Under the instructions of Major-Gen. O. O. Howard, Commissioner of this Bureau, I will lease the land in lots of forty acres, or less, to each refugee or freedman with a family. Under the law, when the term of the lease expires, a title to the amount of land cultivated during the term of the lease can be given by the United States to the lessees.

Associations of freedmen are already forming for the purpose of making the provisions of the law available. An organization known as "The Freedmen's Aid Association," has existed in New Orleans for nearly a year. This body, with others, will give very great assistance in the good work of placing poor white persons and freedmen in a position to become comfortable and prosperous. Much is already due to the Freedmen's Aid Association for important and willing assistance.

CONDUCT OF THE STATE AUTHORITIES.

In regard to the authorities of the State, I can say nothing whatever favorable to the policy of the Government in regard to the freedmen. In all my intercourse with them, I have only been able to discover a spirit of opposition to the proclamation of liberty issued by our late President. The orders of the Commanding General of the Department, the laws of Congress, and the orders of the War Department, have been ignored as far as they could be. Many Judges of Courts have been known to say openly that "they did not want to hear d—d nigger testimony;" and still, for fear of removal by the military commander, they have made an appearance of observing orders and respecting the evidence of the freedmen. But this superficial respect amounts to no more than simply to secure themselves. In most cases the poor people of color were no better off than if a positive refusal to their testimony was given.

EXPENSES FOR THE YEAR.

A detailed statement of the expenses of the Bureau having already been furnished, it is not deemed necessary to present the items in detail for which the money has been expended. A statement is annexed, showing the various sources from which the funds necessary to carry on the work of the Bureau were derived, and the monthly expenses for the half year. The money obtained will be returned to the Departments from which it was borrowed, from the funds which will accrue from the crops on Government colonies, and from those plantations formerly in the hands of the Treasury Department, worked by private parties, in which the Government has a fractional interest. I beg leave to acknowledge my indebtedness to the military authorities for their prompt assistance in furnishing me with funds. Without such assistance, the Bureau could not have succeeded in its work, and much inconvenience to the white and suffering to the black must have ensued. As it was, the Bureau was established on a secure foundation, and has been enabled to meet all the neces-sities of the situation, and has been instrumental in securing happiness to those for whose welfare it was established.

STATEMENT OF EXPENSES, BUREAU OF FREE LABOR, DEPARTMENT OF THE GULF.

1865. RECEIPTS.		
January 1.—Balance from old account	$1,408	33
February 8.—By error in payment Internal Revenue....	10	82
8.—By cash received from Col. H. Robinson, P. M. General	1,106	50
February 21.—By cash received from Col. Stairing, P. M. General......	5,000	00
March 11.—By cash received from Capt. Armstrong, A. Q. M. as per S. O. 67, Ex. 1, H1. Qrs. Dept. of the Gulf	10,000	00
March 16.—By cash received from J. W. Horton for freight paid on supplies......	3	00
March 24.—By cash received from J. Ingraham for forage and care of horses......	48	00
April 7.—By cash received from Col. Holabird per S. O. 93, H1. Qrs. Dept. of the Gulf......	10,000	00
April 8.—By cash received from L. Tregre for forage and care of mules......	16	00
April 13.—By cash received from J. W. Horton for receipts from colony......	169	40
May 9.—By cash received from Capt Armstrong, as per S. O. 121, H1. Qrs. Dept. of the Gulf......	15,000	00
June 3.—By cash received from Capt. Rundle, A. Q. M., as per orders from Gen. Canby, dated May 22 1865....	5,000	00
June 30.—By cash received from J. W. Horton, returned from payment of laborers......	9	00
Total......	$47,771	06

1865. EXPENDITURES.		
February 1.—Expenses of Bureau for month of January	$913	57
March 1.—Expenses of Bureau for month of February	3,721	77
April 1.—Expenses of Bureau for month of March	12,352	85
May 1.—Expenses of Bureau for month of April......	8,233	31
June 1.—Expenses of Bureau for month of May......	11,314	96
July 1.—Expenses of Bureau for month of June......	6,918	65
Balance on hand July 1, 1865......	4,285	95
Total......	$47,771	05

THE RED RIVER SECTION.

As soon as the rebel forces in the Trans-Mississippi Department surrendered, I took measures to establish my assistants in the Red River section, believing that if the affairs of the freedmen were attended to at once, much suffering might be prevented, and much money saved to the Government, which would have to provide for them in case they left their former homes and congregated at the military posts.

The military affairs in this region were under the control of Major-General Herron, who kindly furnished every facility to my assistants to enable them to meet the demands made upon them by the condition of the country, and approved, in orders, the measures suggested by them for the employment and protection of the freedmen. Assistants were appointed at Shreveport, Natchitoches, Alexandria, Monroe, and other important points.

From reports from all of these officers, it is evident that in no part of the State have matters relating to freedmen been managed with more economy to the Government, or more complete success. It will be seen that in whole parishes not a single ration is issued to freedmen by the Government. Extracts from the reports of these officers are herewith submitted :

EXTRACT FROM REPORT OF LIEUT. STICKNEY, ASSISTANT SUPERINTENDENT AT SHREVEPORT.

SHREVEPORT, LA, July 2, 1865.

I have the honor to report, agreeable to instructions, that I arrived here on the 17th ult., after a trip of eight days from New Orleans, and the next day reported to Major-General Herron, commanding Northern Division of Louisiana.

The vast area of the Red River bottom, and the fields upon the uplands, were covered with a luxuriant growth of corn, and as the principal resource of the country was vested in this crop, there seemed to be a general desire to secure as much of it as possible.

Major-General Herron had ordered that written contracts be made, and hundreds of planters came in with as many different forms of agreement. At the same time, the freedmen came forward and stated that they were willing to enter into written agreements, provided that they could be assured that there was no trap laid to ensnare and force them back to slavery.

Meanwhile my office was visited by large numbers daily. The planters came to ascertain what was to be the policy of the Government in regard to the negro, and to acquaint me with his incapacity to take care of himself ; of his indolence, stupidity, his thievish disposition, his utter disregard of all forms of law and order, of the impracticability as well as the impossibility of cultivating the country without some means of "controlling" the persons of laborers. Hundreds of questions were asked, which could all as well have been answered by the inquirer, could he have recognized in the colored laborer a FREE MAN. The freedmen came to me to know whether they were or were not free, and to obtain advice in regard to what it was necessary for them to do. The majority of them I advised to go back to their former homes, and remain there and labor as long as their rights were respected and wages paid them. It gives me great pleasure to state, that at the first of the month there had been drawn no rations from the Government for the support of the freedmen here.

I desire to say that I am under great obligations to Major-General Herron for the kind, cordial and valuable assistance rendered me in carrying out my plans, while he remained in command, and also to Brigadier-General Veatch for the same favors since his arrival here.

EXTRACT FROM ANOTHER REPORT BY THE SAME OFFICER.

I am happy to be able to report that the planters and freedmen in this section are generally entering into written contracts, which are binding for the rest of the year. Where there are many infirm and helple-s to support, and the planter has but a small crop to secure, the contract is for food, clothing, houses, fuel, and medical attendance ; but working hands are receiving as compensation from two to twelve dollars, in money, per month in some cases ; in others from two to thirteen and one-half bushels of corn per month, or a share of the crop, varying, according to circumstances, from 1-14 to ¼ and ½ of the whole amount raised.

There is a great demand for labor now, and there are no idle freedmen about the city. Not a ration has been drawn for any freedman here, except for the sick and attendants at the hospital.

EXTRACT · FROM THE REPORT OF CAPT. FRANK MOREY, ASST. SUPT. FREEDMEN, MONROE, LA.

JULY, 1865.

*   *   *   *   *   *   *   *   *   *

In about two months hence I shall commence fitting up a plantation for a colony. The Pargoud estate, near town, is, I think, abandoned, and will make a fine farm. There will be a great many very old and very young to be taken care of this winter, for many of the best hands in this section were driven off to Texas during the war. I shall have about two thousand contracts made by the 31st inst. There are about twenty-five hundred plantations to put under contract, as near as I can estimate. I have sent agents into the parishes to make contracts, pending the arrival of the Provost Marshals. It is hard to make these people believe that they must *not* pursue the old system of punishment, but they must come to understand that freedom to the slave is an unalterable fact.

EXTRACT FROM REPORT OF LIEUT. L. S. BUTLER, ASST. SUPT. OF FREEDMEN, ALEXANDRIA, LA.

ALEXANDRIA, LA., July 10, 1865.

* * * * * * * *

Some planters seem inclined to treat the freedmen as though they were free, and to pay them their wages, while others talk and act as though they were determined to get their labor for nothing, believing that they will "yet have them back as slaves." An anonymous letter was brought to my notice the other day, *warning parties against hiring these people; threatening the destruction of their property if they do.* I have not yet been able to find out who is the author of it. I mention the circumstance to show you the feeling entertained by some.

What is to be done with minors having neither father nor mother? Also, what is to be done with planters who refuse to hire their former slaves at any price, even when the freedmen are anxious to do so? The brother of Gov. Wells is such a man. His crops are now all "laid by," and he has nothing more to do until it is ready to harvest. His hands have done all they can for a time, and so he wants to send nearly all of them away, retaining enough only of the best ones to harvest his crop when it is ripe. What ought I to do in such a case?

ALABAMA, AND THE WORK IN THAT STATE.

On the   day of   the United States forces under your command occupied the city of Mobile. On the 19th of May, the following order was issued:

HEADQUARTERS, ARMY AND DIVISION OF WEST MISSISSIPPI, Mobile, Ala,, May 19, 1865.

GENERAL FIELD ORDERS No. 28. -

MR. THOMAS W. CONWAY, General Superintendent of Freedmen, Department of the Gulf, will take charge of the freedmen in and around Mobile. Such officers as he may appoint will draw the necessary supplies from the Commissary and Quartermaster's Department, upon requisitions approved by the Commander of the Post. Supplies not furnished by these Departments, will be procured from funds in the hands of Mr. CONWAY.

All persons formerly held as slaves will be treated in every respect as entitled to the rights of freedmen, and such as desire their services will be required to pay for them.

Care will be taken not to disturb abruptly the connections now existing, and all colored persons having places or employment are advised to remain, whenever the persons by whom they are employed recognize their rights and agree to compensate them for their services.

All unemployed colored persons will report at once at the office established for the care of freedmen, for the purpose of having their names and residences registered, and being provided with employment. Those employed by the Government will be regularly enrolled, subsisted and paid. Copies of the rolls of those employed in the different departments of the army will be furnished the Superintendent of Freedmen, and when discharged from that employment will be directed to report to the Superintendent.

By order of Major-General E. R. S. CANBY:

C. T. CHRISTENSEN,
Lt. Colonel, Ass't Adjutant General.

I immediately assumed the duties imposed on me by this order, and devoted myself to the task of providing for the great number of freedmen who had flocked to our lines, and were without shelter, or even food to maintain them from day to day.

I found the freedmen well disposed, and apparently desired nothing to quiet their apprehensions but an assurance, from some one they could trust, that the freedom guaranteed to them by the Emancipation Proclamation was a fact, and that the whole power of the United States would protect them in the enjoyment of their liberty. I adopted such measures as would tend to check idleness, and secure the labor of those able to work. I took particular pains to assure them on the subject of their freedom ; and notwithstanding their sudden transition from the condition of slaves to freemen, I had the satisfaction of seeing both white and black adapting themselves to the new order of things, and all the measures taken by me for the education and elevation of the freedmen are progressing finely.

The surrender of the rebel forces under General Dick Taylor, placed the Gulf States again under the control of the Government. The following letter of instructions was received by me :

HEADQUARTERS, ARMY AND DIVISION OF WEST MISSISSIPPI, }
    Mobile, Ala., May 22, 1865.   · }

Sir—The Major-General Commanding directs that you proceed to Montgomery, Ala., and such other interior points as you may find it necessary or expedient to visit, for the purpose of giving your personal supervision to the arrangements that may be adopted for the care and support of freedmen within the limits of this command, and not already provided for in the Department of the Gulf and Mississippi.

The provisions of General Orders No. 13, from these Headquarters, of General Order No. 23, from Headquarters, Department of the Gulf, and of the enclosed memoranda, will govern, so far as they may be found applicable to the circumstances of the locality and the present condition of the planters and the colored people.

The Major General Commanding does not consider it necessary to give you detailed instructions, which might possibly embarrass your action, and he relies implicitly upon your knowledge of the subject, and your judgement, to make the best arrangements that can be made.

Very respectfully, your obedient servant.

C. T. CHRISTENSEN,
    Lieut. Colonel and Assistant Adjutant General.

Thomas W. Conway, Esq., General Superintendent Bureau of Free Labor, Mobile, Alabama.

MEMORANDA.

HEADQUARTERS, MILITARY DIVISION OF WEST MISSISSIPPI, }
    New Orleans, La., May, 1865.   }

All persons formerly held as slaves will be treated in every respect as entitled to the rights of freedmen, and such as desire their services will be required to pay for them. Care will be taken not to disturb abruptly the connections now existing, and all colored persons having places of employment are advised to remain, wherever the persons by whom they are employed recognize their rights and agree to compensate them for their services.

Until the regulations to be established by the Bureau of Freedmen at Washington have been promulgated and applied, the following provisional regulations will be enforced in the limits of this command, except that in districts where the system promulgated in General Order No. 13, of February 1, 1865, has been applied, no change will be made; and the general provisions of that system will be extended, as far as the circumstances of the case make them applicable.

1. Planters, and all persons engaged in industrial pursuits, may hire the number of colored men they desire to employ, on such terms and conditions as the parties may agree upon. The contract must, in all cases, be reduced to writing, and a copy furnished the person employed. It must state distinctly whether the consideration is to be paid in money or in a share of the products raised, and must be approved by the Assistant Superintendent of Freedmen in whose District the transaction takes place. In addition to this consideration, the employer will furnish the person hired with good lodgings, fuel, food, clothing, and medical attendance.

2. Contracts will be made to the 31st of December proximo. After that date, new contracts must be made, if desired.

3. Mr. Thomas W. Conway, General Superintendent of Freedmen of the Department of the Gulf, will also have general charge of the freedmen in the States of Mississippi and Alabama, and such other localities as are or may be occupied by troops belonging to this command, and will establish branch offices in all principal localities, giving to his Assistants, in addition to the general rules necessary for their guidance, such special instructions as will secure to colored employées protection in their rights as freedmen, and tend to make them appreciate their new privileges and obligations in all the relations of life.

The officers appointed by him will draw the necessary supplies from the Commissary and Quartermaster's Departments, upon requisitions approved by the respective post commanders. Supplies not furnished by these Departments will be procured from the funds in the hands of Mr. Conway.

4. All unemployed colored persons will report at once, at either of the offices established for the care of freedmen, for the purpose of having their names registered, and being provided with employment. Those employed by the Government will be regularly enrolled, subsisted and paid. Copies of the rolls of those employed in the different departments of the army will be furnished the respective Assistant Superintendents of Freedmen, to whom all persons discharged from such employment will be directed to report.

5. Agents will at once be sent into the interior for the purpose of explaining to the planters and the freedmen the new relations that now exist between

them, and to facilitate such measures as may be necessary to secure the growing crops, and avert the danger of scarcity and famine.

6. Commanding officers are directed to furnish every facility and assistance that may be required to the officers charged with the execution of this order, and the rules that are now, and may hereafter be, established by the General Superintendent of Freedmen.

A true copy. Attest:

C. T. CHRISTENSEN,
Lieutenant Colonel and Assistant Adjutant General.

In accordance with my instructions I began a tour of inspection through the State, to enable me to form a just conception of the wants of the freedmen.

I visited the main points on the Mobile and Great Northern Railroad, where I found much misery and suffering. In some cases I found white men, returned rebels, who were being supported by the blacks who were formerly their slaves. I appointed the following officers as my assistants, and located them at the following towns:

George A. Harmount, late Lieutenant Colonel 97th U. S. C. I., Assistant Superintendent for city of Mobile and vicinity.

Capt. H. M. Crydenwise, 73d U. S. C. I., Assistant Superintendent for Demopolis, Ala., and vicinity.

Chaplain S. S. Gardner, 73d U. S. C. I., Assistant Superintendent for Selma, Ala., and vicinity.

Chaplain C. W. Buckley, Assistant Superintendent for Montgomery, Ala., and vicinity.

These gentlemen entered upon their duties, having their headquarters as above, but extending their labors through the surrounding country, addressing the freedmen, explaining to them the nature of their situation, and impressing upon their minds the necessity for them to labor and support themselves and families; that idleness would be considered a crime and could not be tolerated. I was quite fortunate in securing the services of such valuable assistants; their hearts were in their work, and they entered into it with their might. The result of their labors is most flattering to them and constitutes their best reward.

The labor system, which had proved so successful in the State of Louisiana, was adopted in Alabama, and planters, to some extent, showed a creditable spirit, and seemed willing and anxious to secure the services of their former slaves, upon contracts securing to the freedmen compensation, food, medical attendance and a comfortable home. The Assistant Superintendents visited the plantations and witnessed these contracts, protecting the freedmen from fraud and imposition.

OUTRAGES UPON FREEDMEN.

Many cases of outrages upon freedmen occurred prior to the establish-

4

ment of my assistants throughout the State, but in most cases they were found to be the doings of lawless and wicked men—the same material that furnished the guerilla parties of the late army of the insurgents—and not sanctioned by the intelligent and respectable portion of the community. In every instance of this kind measures were promptly taken to arrest the offenders and bring them to justice, and where necessary the military authorities were called upon for assistance. In all cases such assistance was cheerfully given.

The prejudice against the negro may be as strong as ever, but the prompt and energetic measures taken at the outset to redress any wrongs committed upon freedmen has had its effect, and I am most happy to say that instances of oppression, injustice and wrong are becoming more and more rare every day.

Matters were progressing very satisfactorily in the State, and improving daily at the time of the transfer of the affairs of the freedmen to the Commissioner of the Bureau of Refugees, Freedmen and Abandoned Lands appointed for the State.

The following extracts from reports of my assistants are respectfully submitted as indicative of the progress and condition of affairs in their respective districts:

EXTRACT FROM REPORT OF CAPT. II. M. CRYDENWISE, ASSISTANT SUPERINTENDENT AT DEMOPOLIS, ALA.

Office of Assistant Superintendent of Freedmen, ⎰
Demopolis, Ala., June 20, 1865. ⎱

Mr. T. W. Conway, Gen'l Sup't of Freedmen, Dep't of the Gulf:

Sir—I have the honor to make the following tri-monthly report of my duty or action as Assistant Superintendent of Freedmen for Demopolis and vicinity for the ten days ending June 20, 1865.

Finding it necessary to have more than one plantation as a Home Colony, I have leased another for the remainder of the year. This plantation contains about one thousand acres of land. There are on the plantation about three hundred and forty acres of corn, ninety acres of cotton, pea patch, potatoes' etc. I take everything growing on the plantation, and give as hire twenty-five hundred bushels of corn and one-half of all cotton grown. I made an inventory of the farming implements, stock, etc., left on the place, with the assessed value of each, and am to return the same when the plantation is turned over.

Everything is working quite as well as I could hope. I have held meetings at Era, Greensborough, Morristown and Dayton. These were very largely attended, and much interest manifested.

There are at present on the two plantations about two hundred of those who could not care for themselves. This number is increasing.

Very respectfully, your obedient servant,
II. M. CRYDENWISE,
Captain and Assistant Superintendent Freedmen.

BUREAU OF FREE LABOR, }
Montgomery, Alabama, June 1, 1865. }

T. W. CONWAY, General Superintendent Freedmen :

Sir—I have the honor to submit the following report of the working of the Free Labor system under my supervision for the month ending 31st day of May, 1865.

As this is the first report that will come under your notice from this section, and as the system is not yet fully inaugurated, this report must resemble, of necessity, an extended letter more than an official communication.

ASSEMBLIES OF COLORED PEOPLE.

On Saturday, 27th ult., the day after your departure, I sent for a delegation of the principal men, including the pastors, from each of the colored congregations in the city. I explained to them my relations to their race, and appointed an hour at which I would occupy their pulpits, and in the course of my sermon explained and read your labor regulations. On the next day (Sunday) I spoke three times to not less than two thousand colored people. I told them plainly that they were free, and that the Government would maintain their freedom. No abuse, no personal violence, no selling, no buying, no breaking up families by force would be allowed.

They were *not* free to be insolent, to be idle, to pilfer, to steal, or do anything contrary to good order. They were free to come under the *restraints of law* ; free to toil and claim the fruits of their own industry. At the same time I pressed upon their minds the binding nature of contracts and the vast importance of at once seeking employment. They received it all with joy, and the effect has been most happy. The city has been far more quiet, many less idlers in the streets, and mutual confidence between employers and the freedmen, on a just basis, has been created.

During the day I met several of the clergymen of the place, who waited upon me on Monday morning last, and owing to the pressure of business at the time an interview was appointed for the evening. After tea they called at my office, and we entered into a conversation which lasted till midnight. I talked plainly and earnestly with them, and finally, when we parted, they pledged all the assistance in their power to aid in carrying out our new system. They asked many questions in a captious spirit, which were answered with the conscious feeling that the *right* and the *power* were and are on my side.

Upon the whole our interview was cordial, and I never felt more satisfied with my success in defending the right and justice of our course.

THE PLANTERS.

Planters from all sections have rushed to this office to ask countless questions about contracts. Our method is so different from anything they have been accustomed to that they cannot comprehend it at first. Many of them are men of limited business experience, accustomed to raising corn and cotton by slave labor. They have shown much candor in most cases, and have asked their thousands of questions from a sincere desire to know what we wished them to do, and that they might be right. In all such cases I have answered their questions with great patience and fulness till my tired lungs pain me. But few have shown any disposition to treat the freedmen unjustly. In one instance I refused to let one man hire freedmen. But he soon came to terms.

ORDER IN THE COUNTRY DISTRICTS.

In a number of cases I have furnished guards for plantations, where the freedmen were disorderly. Their presence restored order at once. This necessity has now passed away and order is being rapidly restored, and vagrancy is much diminished. In some cases, where disorder was reported, I have sent an officer to investigate the cause, and, if possible, settle the disturbance.

GOVERNMENT PLANTATIONS.

I have been delayed in securing plantations upon which to work our idle hands to-day. This delay was caused by my inability to get a report from Headquarters. I have now authority to use such abandoned plantations as I may select. I have selected such plantations as have crops already in the ground. I have done so for two reasons: 1st, There is a risk in planting at this late season unless the soil is *well adapted to late crops*. A crop planted now would probably be light. The result, I think, would be better if I were to expend our labor on corn now a foot high, even if I were to give a small portion of crop for rent, than to plant now and pay no rent.

2d. We have not the stock to plow the ground. We have not been able yet to draw a team for our own use. So I have selected two thousand acres of land now planted to corn. which I intend to work with the hands whom we are now feeding and hold in idleness. I hope this will meet with your approval. The proposition I telegraphed to you but failed to get a reply.

CONDITION OF THE CAMP.

The camp remains unchanged—some going, some coming, constantly. The aggregate is 3200. Sickness is light, though our surgeon is nearly out of medicine. A requisition was approved to-day, and more will be drawn as soon as medicines arrive at the Post.

Our surgeon ought to have more help. I shall make an effort to this effect. The camp will be much decreased, as to-morrow. after rations are drawn, some will be taken to plantations. I shall also need more help at the office.

I wish very much that First Lieutenant A. R. Mills, 47th Regiment U. S Colored Infantry, might be detailed to record the contracts made with planters. He would be an excellent man for the purpose.

At first the planters seemed anxious to have the freedmen removed from their plantations, but they have changed their policy now, and retain all they can support, even keeping the aged and helpless children. This is accounted for in two ways. 1st, Through attachment in many cases. 2d. Through fear of scarcity of labor the coming year, and the planters are willing to keep more than they want this year for the sake of having them another year on their plantations, ready to be hired at the opening of the season.

A few are so deluded and so inseparably connected with the cursed institution of slavery that they think the institution will be revived some day, and God will give them their rights.

CITY PASSES.

I have two clerks who spend their whole time in giving out city passes upon printed blanks. These are citizen clerks, and, being acquainted with the people of the place, know whose certificates are reliable.

CONCLUSION.

I hardly know how I am going to enforce the regulations in districts remote from the city. Men come here from a distance of seventy and a hundred miles. My time will be entirely occupied here in the office for some weeks yet. I shall, however, take short trips into the country soon, talking to the colored people on large plantations and in small towns. Society never existed in such a chaotic state as here. No law, no order. To bring good order out of such confusion is a work from which one of my capacity might well shrink. Yet I am sustained by the thought that nothing is denied to well devoted labor. My days and nights have been given up to the urgent demands of my situation.

Hoping I may be able in my next report to convince you of progress in our work.

I remain, very respectfully,

Your obedient servant,

(Signed)   C. W. BUCKLEY,

Assistant Superintendent of Freedmen.

BUREAU OF FREE LABOR,
Montgomery, Alabama. July 1, 1865.

T. W. CONWAY, General Superintendent of Freedmen :

Sir—I have the honor herewith to submit my report for the month ending June 30th, 1865.

The past month has been one of great change in many respects. The condition of country districts, as well as the order and industry of the city, has vastly improved. There is much less vagrancy on the part of freedmen, and far less abuse and ill-treatment on the part of their late masters. Since the publication of President Johnson's Amnesty Proclamation, and since his interviews with different delegations from Southern States have been made public, our citizens have been more open and frank to acknowledge that slavery is forever dead.

Some relinquish their hold reluctantly, and are hardly willing to bury the corpse from their sight. A few, the more rebellious, prefer to kill the negro than to see him free. But events hasten. Our victory urges on to new achievements. Those who one week ago yielded up their slaves to freedom, and accepted the new order of things with cheerfulness, are now agitated afresh by fears of negro suffrage. Thus it is by the will of Heaven, by Divine right, that the nation's freedmen are coming, surely and speedily, to occupy their rightful position —equality with white men in the eyes of the law

HOME COLONY.

The application for the assignment of lands to be used temporarily for the colored people made by you to the military authorities, was returned to me on June 7th, designating seven plantations which might be rendered serviceable for our purpose. I at once examined these plantations, and moved from camp two hundred and fifty persons upon one of them, in order to save the crop, as the season for corn culture was rapidly passing away, this being the only crop of any importance raised in this portion of the State. Two other plantations, as we were moving on to them, were released and given back to the owners. Afterwards two more were released. One other was so near town as to be unserviceable to us, as straggling into and out of town would greatly annoy us, and disturb the industry of the place.

This left us with but two plantations under our control, and one of these was small, having but few quarters, no house, water scarce and poor, crop small, and on the whole useless for our purpose. I decided not to use it. We have, therefore, held on to the first place, embracing one thousand acres, and saved about five hundred acres of corn. But owing to the fact that the corn was entirely neglected in the early part of the season, when it ought to have been worked, coupled with a severe drouth, and being unable to draw any mules, General Smith having given out to citizens all his old stock before my arrival here, our farming operations will not be so successful and profitable as I could wish. Had we commenced our operations on May 1st, instead of June 1st, our results would have been far more encouraging. In the meantime, while some have been engaged in agriculture, others have been busy erecting cheap and plain houses at the Home Colony to protect women and helpless children against the coming fall and winter storms. This undertaking has been delayed for the want of a sufficient number of common tools. Lately, however, the Post Quartermaster turned over to me fifty axes, and before this report shall have reached you, the last vestage of the freedmen's camp across the river will be broken up, and they, with the unemployed negroes in town, will be made comfortable on the plantation eight miles from the city.

I have made extra effort to remove this camp before, but I saw no object in moving it till I could improve the comfort of the colored people in it ; and as we have been unable to draw teams for our own use. I have thought, while dependent upon the teams of the Post for hauling our rations, etc., it was not practicable to make the change till we could profit by so doing. The time has now come when we can make the change with safety and comfort.

HOSPITALS.

Application for lumber sufficient to build, at the Home Colony, a plain and commodious hospital for such sick as fall upon our hands, has been made. We now wait the reply. It is very difficult to procure buildings, either in the city or in the adjoining country, for hospital purposes.

We greatly need a building where small children can be provided for during the sickness of parents. As we are now situated, it often happens that a mother is taken sick having two or three small children, who are obliged to go to the hospital with her, for she has no one to care for them in her absence. Had we a place to put such children till the mother recovers, it would relieve the hospital, and be far better for the children.

An Orphan Asylum is also greatly needed. The number of children is very great, and among them many orphans. I am located in a section where negroes were regarded as the most popular and profitable mode of investing capital. They were always saleable. There are hundreds of plantations in this section whose only net profits consisted in the increase and growth of negro children. This being the case, vast numbers of children, helpless and friendless, must be cared for. The demands for an Asylum are urgent, and I hope before fall to establish one. If an appeal were made to the benevolence of the North, I doubt not sufficient aid could be obtained.

The liberal aid I have received from Hon. James Yeatman, President of the Western Sanitary Commission, and Hon. Francis George Shaw, President of the National Freedmen's Relief Association, New York city, for similar purposes in other sections, renders me confident of material support in this instance.

MARRIAGE CERTIFICATES.

Feeling the necessity of regulating the connubial relations of the freedmen, I have inaugurated a system by which an accurate record is kept of all lawful marriages, and certificates are issued to the married parties.

The annexed circular will explain my method :

BUREAU OF FREE LABOR,
Montgomery, Ala., July 3, 1865.

CIRCULAR No. 2.

That freedmen may acquire proper views of the sacred nature and solemn obligations of the marriage rite, thereby promoting the virtue and future welfare of the race, blank marriage certificates will hereafter be issued from this office. Attached to each certificate is an accompanying return, which, after being filled out by the officiating person, will be returned by him without delay for registration. Thus an accurate marriage record will be kept for future referencece.

Chaplains in the army, clergymen and magistrates, are earnestly invited to authorize the marriages of such as have been living together as husband and wife, and to encourage lawful marriage in all cases among candidates for matrimony. Each ceremony should be witnessed by a person who can sign his name in writing, and not by mark.

Care should be taken to impress upon the minds of candidates, the solemn nature of their marriage vows, and to add such instructions as shall lead them to order aright their households, making them, as far as possible, the abodes of industry, peace, and Christian faith.

[Signed]   C. W. BUCKLEY,
                                Assistant Superintendent of Freedmen.

RESIGNATION.

Capt. A. L. Brown, A. A. Q. M. of this Department, handed in a request to be relieved, assigning as his reason that he was not contented with his situation. I approved and forwarded it, as I am confident that a man to be useful in this department must take a deep and abiding interest in his work, and feel that his toil is not drudgery. One should be sustained and animated by the thought that he is giving his energies to the welfare of an oppressed race. My relations with Captain Brown have been cordial from the beginning. and I fear it will be difficult to fill his place.

CONDUCT OF FREEDMEN.

War naturally arouses and quickens the energies of a nation, and gives a wonderful impulse to national life. These Southern States give striking evidences of the truthfulness of this statement. The energy with which the inhabitants meet the emergencies of the rebellion was worthy of a nobler cause. But the quickening influences of war have not been felt by the white race only. The energies of the colored race have been aroused and called forth. Superadded to the vivifying effects of war, is the inspiration of a newly acquired freedom. The future to them is radient with new hopes. As the burden of slavery is lifted, their purposes rise accordingly. Already two colored schools are in progress, and largely attended. These schools are self-supporting. Children of color walk our streets with books under their arms, notwithstanding it is contrary to the statute laws of the State to teach a colored child to read.

The general conduct of freedmen is good. In many cases they receive nothing more than a support for their work. The plantations of many of their former owners have been so desolated by war that nothing but a support will be made. Citizens who are unwilling to adopt themselves to the new order of things, find but little trouble in controlling their help. There are a few citizens in every neighborhood who cause trouble, but freedmen are not ill-treated as much as one month ago.

PETITIONS.

Petitions, through military channels, constantly come in for aid to regulate freedmen's affairs. The last from the citizens of Girard, Ala., opposite Columbus. This makes our field of operations very large, especially for our limited help. We are looking forward with hope to the early arrival of the Assistant Commissioner of the State.

Montgomery being the capital of the State, and the largest city in this portion of the State, it is natural for business to centre here; and the manner in which things are done here, will give shape to similar transactions in other sections. Realizing this fact, I have endeavored to act with caution and deliberation. My experience thus far, confirms my belief in the ultimate success of our system. In the contest between slave and free labor, the issue is not doubtful to my mind.

These broad fields, now desolated and neglected, will be made to yield a more bountiful harvest than ever before. The lost millions, accumulated by years of unrequited toil, will be replaced; but it will be by the industry of well directed free labor.

I have the honor to be, with much respect,

Your obedient servant,

C. W. BUCKLEY,
Assistant Superintendent of Freedmen.

REPORT OF CHAPLAIN GARDNER, ASSISTANT SUPERINTENDENT AT SELMA, ALA.

SELMA, ALA., June 12, 1865.

MR. THOMAS W. CONWAY, General Superintendent of Freedmen:

Dear Sir—I will write you a few lines unofficially, to give and get information. You ask in your telegram if the freedmen are persecuted. I think not, in the majority of instances They have come in from some plantations with stories of cutting and slaying, as they call it, but generally the planters have shown a disposition to meet us in good faith, and deal fairly with the people. General Wilson stripped almost every plantation in this vicinity of its stock, so that, as an average, not more than a half crop can be raised. Under these circumstances, connected with the utter collapse of the Confederate currency, I have approved many contracts in which labor was exchanged for subsistence, clothes, home, and medical attendance. Many more, however, have given a share of the crop, usually a fifth or fourth. There are questions of practical dealing arising continually, which, in the absence of any specific rules or definite instructions, I endeavor to decide in accordance with the general principles of the Regulations, in the light of justice and common sense.

Some cavilling and mean planter will take his stand upon the declared freedom of the slave, and argue that the release of obligations is mutual, hence he may send from his place the infirm, the unemployed women—in short the non-productive hands, and hire the productive. I have decided that families must not be separated ; and where wages cannot be paid, all the support of an average assortment of hands must be offset against the labor of all.

In the future, when full wages are paid, the producing hands in a family will support the non-producing. Some, too, are sending off a portion of their hands now, after the bulk of the work upon the growing crop is completed. They have been notified that the labor of the agricultural year will entitle the laborer to support through the agricultural year. There are a few instances in which the blacks are reported to have gained an ascendancy over the owner by terror, and are living riotously and wastefully upon the plantation. I go to-day to investigate one of these.

There seems to be no other way to secure the crop, or the safety of the neighborhood. or the integrity of other laborers in the vicinity, but to keep a guard there permanently until order is restored. In many cases it is the result of criminal folly on the part of soldiers, in telling them absurd stories about their condition as freedmen, and the mere announcement of the truth from an authoritative source will bring them to order.

A case has come to me to-day like this : the owner of slaves had hired them out, cultivating no place himself, but keeping the non-productive children at his quarters. At the change, the hired hands scatter about and leave their children upon their former owner. Can I allow food to those children until we get a Home Colony? Or shall I order him to maintain them? We have no place to keep them consistent with humanity.

The employers sometimes complain that the hands will not work, even after the contract, and only a half or third is accomplished in the same time that used to be. In consultation with Col. Marshall, Post Commander, an excellent man. I have decided that such discipline as would be considered mild and humane under the old plan might be used, especially with the young and thoughtless. If rations are withheld as a punishment, they kill stock and make bad worse.

The application for the designation of a site for a Home Colony, was made the first day after I received your telegram. As yet, however, I have learned nothing as to its progress. Time fails me to mention other points.

Very respectfully, your obedient servant,

SAML. S. GARDNER,
Assistant Superintendent of Freedmen.

COLORED SOLDIERS APPLYING FOR LAND.

One of the regiments of United States Colored Infantry in this Department has fifty thousand dollars set apart for the purpose of purchasing four or five of the largest plantations on the Mississippi. I understand that several other regiments are making similar arrangements. I believe that in the State of Louisiana there are about twenty regiments of these troops. These regiments could purchase every inch of confiscated and abandoned land in the hands of the Government in this State. If their commanding officers will give the subject some attention J am quite certain that the result will be such as will secure to this class of our soldiery a lasting benefit, which will do more than anything else to secure for themselves and their children a place and a character in society which cannot be had in any other manner.

I am in constant receipt of communications from companies and squads of these soldiers applying for such portions of land as they consider themselves able to purchase and cultivate. This interest in the soil is general with these soldiers. At the expiration of their terms of service they all want small farms. Many of the letters which I receive speak very confidently of the expected results. Some soldiers say that they have wives who are willing to work; others that their whole families are able and anxious to help them. Some have saved five hundred dollars, others two hundred, and so on. I see no intention among any of these men to live otherwise than industriously. Indeed the spirit which they manifest is commendable to a high degree.

HELP FROM THE MILITARY.

To the Commander of the Department; to Brevet Major General T. W. Sherman; to nearly all the Post and District Commanders, I am indebted for most cordial assistance in my work. The military assistance rendered, has enabled me to feel, that in no State in the South are the interests of the freedmen and those of agriculture more advanced than in Louisiana.

CONCLUSION.

In concluding this Report I beg leave to call your attention to the increasing efforts and general disposition of the old slaveholders to have this Bureau discontinued. The Press of the State is almost universally opposed to it. The people, excepting, of course, the truly loyal, are determined to " manage and control the negroes" to their own liking. Allow me to give you reasons why

THIS BUREAU SHOULD BE CONTINUED.

1. If discontinued, twenty thousand children, freed by the Government in this State, would be turned out of their schools, their teachers, numbering more than three hundred, would be forced to abandon their philanthropic labors, and the doors of more than one hundred school-houses would be closed.

2. The colored people of the State, under the weight of oppressive vagrant laws, the force of constant opposition to their liberty, and the endless persecutions and sufferings inflicted by their late owners, would as certainly be exterminated as that night follows the day ; and those who would not die

would emigrate either to Mexico, to which country most of the freedmen of Louisiana would go, or to the Northern States. This would be injustice to them on which the vengeance of Heaven would assuredly fall. It would be a wrong to the State which at present appears to be omitted from the calculations of all who speak upon the subject. The only available laboring class for the soil of Louisiana would pass away in ten years or less; and history could not furnish an evidence of any such injustice perpetrated by any Government as that which our Government would perpetrate upon a people whose freedom it ordained without having the moral stamina to maintain it, or the honesty to carry it on to perfection.

3. The law of Congress, act March 3, 1864, would be a farce and a failure. The land allotted to freedmen by that law could never be occupied or used. No colored person could cultivate an inch of ground in his own name or for his own benefit.

4. The Proclamation of Emancipation which, in the hands and by the labors of this Bureau, has proved so wise and glorious a measure, would fail in its purposes, and oppressive local laws would suspend the blessed results now enjoyed by this people as fruits of that immortal document.

5. Society, which has already hardly recovered from the temper which moved it to violent rebellion against the Government of the Union, would continue disorganized and disgraced by outrages and crimes too shocking to contemplate. Already the Bureau has all it can do to suppress slave ordinances and codes in conflict with the liberty proclaimed by the President's Proclamations, the laws of Congress, the orders of General Howard and of the Commander of the Department. Some magistrates deny the testimony of freedmen. Others would be glad to do so but they fear the consequences.

6. The old and helpless freedmen of the State, who have labored all their lives to cut down the forests of Louisiana; to enrich both their masters and the State; whose toils have only been rewarded with stripes and lashes, would be left uncared for, and as only fit to drop into their graves.

7. The United States Government, whose decrees have given liberty to the former slaves of the insurgent States, cannot now abandon its own policy or leave those whom it has freed to the mercy of those from whose grasp it has taken them, at least till such time as the power derived by owning property, by education, and by having the right of suffrage, will give them a secure position in which they can defend their own liberty exactly as the white man defends his.

I give these expressions seriously. I know whereof I speak. More than four years have been faithfully devoted to the problem which the Government has committed to this Bureau for solution. I am fully acquainted with the people of this State. They have some noble qualities. They are, however, not yet fit to be trusted with the defence of the liberty of the freedmen. They will not be in less than three or five years. In that time the freedmen will own land, they will vote, and, as a consequence, they can take care of themselves. At that time the Bureau can discontinue its labors. If it is forced to do so before, the results will be heartrending.

Justice to the freedmen, the interest of the Government, the prosperity of the State, the cause of religion and humanity, all call upon us to give to this subject wise and timely attention. By so doing very dangerous consequences will be avoided.

INSURRECTION.

The freedmen will not engage in any insurrection against the State, or any portion of it. The white population have the character of insurgents exclusively to themselves in this portion of our country. The colored population live much under the control of the Christian religion, and they have no disposition to murder or destroy. They are peaceable, forgiving, merciful. If they are not protected in the enjoyment of the liberty proclaimed to them, they will go away from the country, trusting in God.

I have the honor to be, General,

Very respectfully,

Your obedient servant,

THOMAS W. CONWAY,

Assistant Commissioner, Bureau of Refugees,

Freedmen and Abandoned Lands,

State of Louisiana.

Late General Superintendent of Freedmen,

Department of the Gulf.

[SEE APPENDIX ON NEXT PAGE.]

APPENDIX.

Note 1.—On the sixteenth page of this report, there occurs this sentence, which appears by mistake: "The character of both State and city officials is pleasing to contemplate." It was intended to have said: "The *conduct* of both State and city officials is not pleasing to contemplate."

Note 2.—The National Freedmen's Relief Association, of which Hon. Francis George Shaw is President, has rendered a service to this Bureau in every way, which cannot be too warmly appreciated. Ship loads of clothing to cover the nakedness of poor freedmen, have been sent by this Society, to be scattered to the needy along the Alabama and Red Rivers, and many thousands have been helped in their distresses.

The Northwestern Freedmen's Aid Commission, of which Rev. Jacob R. Shepard is President, has been prompt to aid the Bureau in relieving the wants of the suffering, and the people for whose special benefit that society is established. This Society was the first to plant the banner of free education in Alabama, and its agents were untiring, faithful men. Their work is now progressing.